# Contents

# Brecht, Bertolt (1898–1956)

German poet, theorist, stage director, playwright, Bertolt Brecht was born on February 10, 1898, the son of a Protestant father (Berthold Brecht) and a Catholic mother (née Sophie Brezing) at Auf dem Rain 7, Augsburg, Bavaria. He was christened Eugen Berthold Friedrich. Berthold Sr. worked at the Heindel paper factory in Augsburg and was eventually to be its managing director. Both parents hailed from Achern in the Black Forest. Brecht attended the Volksschule from 1904 to 1908 and the Realgymnasium from 1908 to 1917. The author's own account (in a letter to the critic Herbert Ihering):

> Elementary school bored me for four years. During nine years of being lulled to sleep at the Augsburg Realgymnasium I didn't manage to be very much help to my teachers.

But by 1913 he was a published writer of remarkable accomplishment, as both prose and verse printed in the school paper, *Die Ernte* (The Harvest), attest. His first play, *The Bible,* appeared there in January 1914. In this year, Brecht came before a general public, starting to publish in the *Augsburger Neueste Nachrichten.* Some of the Brecht items in this paper are nationalistic. The young poet steps forth as the patriot of Kaiser Wilhelm's war. Yet at least one commentator has questioned the sincerity of the nationalism, in view of poems stating other attitudes, and in view of the greater sophistication of the standpoint in items written earlier. By 1916, certainly, the profile of the Brecht the world knows is clearly seen in such a poem as "The Song of the Fort Donald Railroad Gang," as remarkable a work as any eighteen year old, except Rimbaud, has ever been known to write.

Graduating from high school in 1917, Brecht continued to live at home (Bleichstrasse 2, Augsburg) while beginning to study medicine in nearby Munich. He was even able to stay in Augsburg when inducted into the army in 1918, his service being limited to the duties of a medical orderly in the local barracks. (The story that he acted as a surgeon and actually amputated limbs is a legend created by Brecht himself.) His famous poem "Legend of the Dead Soldier" dates from this period; it was to be the only work of his cited by the Nazis as their reason for depriving him of German citizenship in 1935. This was also the year he wrote his first mature play, *Baal.* It was too indecent to find any immediate producer. Brecht's father offered to pay for it to be printed but only on a condition his son did not accept: that the family name not appear in the volume.

Though peace had come to the world, 1919 was a year of the greatest storm and stress for Germany and for Bertolt Brecht. It was in this year that he had his first taste of politics, and his only direct contact with revolution, the unsuccessful revolution which his native Bavaria underwent. He belonged for a time to the Augsburg Soldiers' Soviet and to the Independent Social Democratic Party. That bitter disenchantment followed is indicated in the play which grew out of this chapter in his life, *Drums in the Night,* as well as in the poem "Ballad of the Red Army Soldier" (the "Red Army" of this work was almost certainly the Bavarian, not the Russian one). This was also the time of a love affair with a girl called Bie Banholzer, who bore him a son. (He was named Frank, after Wedekind, but was later consigned to an orphanage and was finally killed on the Russian front in World War II.) Nineteen nineteen was an *annus mirabilis* for Bertolt Brecht the poet. Though not all the products of his pen from this time have survived, many of the poems published later in *Manual of Piety* were written then.

In 1920 Brecht's mother died. His poem on the event expresses heartbreak in a remarkably direct way. It was at this point that he moved from Augsburg to Munich (Akademiestrasse 15). The Munich years were marked by a close friendship with the playwright Arnolt Bronnen (later a Nazi, later still a communist sympathizer), by marriage to Marianne Zoff, daughter of a Munich theater man, and by the birth of Brecht's first legitimate child, Hanne (later the actress Hanne Hiob, an occasional guest artist with the Berlin Ensemble). In these years, too, Brecht not only wrote plays but had them produced. Here the principal event was the production of *Drums in the Night* at the Munich Kammerspiele in 1922, which led to Brecht's being awarded the Kleist Prize through the influence of the critic Herbert Ihering. The first productions of *Jungle of*

*Cities* (also called *In the Swamp*) in 1923, and of *Edward II* in 1924, were less successful with the public and the critics but equally important for the young playwright.

In 1924 Brecht settled in Berlin (Spichernstrasse 19). His first marriage fell apart, and in 1926 Brecht had a son, Stefan, by the actress Helene Weigel, whom he married two years later and stayed married to for the rest of his life. It was in this period that Brecht found his way to the kind of drama he intended to create, the play *A Man's a Man* making the decisive breakthrough from his early manner (lyric, balladesque, expressionistic) to what he was to call Epic Theater (narrative, objective, political, didactic). And this achievement was by no means a purely aesthetic matter. In October 1926, he wrote to a friend: "I am eight feet deep in *Das Kapital.*" It was also his habit to seek out personal mentors, and two such were important at this stage: the left-wing, but not strictly Marxian, sociologist Fritz Sternberg and the Marxian, but anti–Communist Party, Karl Korsch.

The early plays and the publication in 1927 of his book of poems *Manual of Piety* gave Brecht a solid reputation in literary circles. His work reached a wider public for the first time with the Berlin production of *The Threepenny Opera* at the Schiffbauerdamm Theater (première: August 28, 1928). The now world-famous "musical" not only stayed in the repertoire of that theater until the advent of Hitler, when all such works were banned, but was played all over Germany and Central Europe generally. Two successful films were promptly made from it on the same set, one French, one German. But success stopped at the water's edge. *The Threepenny Opera* was not to be done in London until after World War II. In 1933 it ran briefly (twelve performances) at the Empire Theater in New York and was not even a *succès d'estime.*

The money Brecht made from *The Threepenny Opera* bought him the time to write less successful works. *Happy End* (1929) was a flop (and mainly by Elisabeth Hauptmann), but it was also the starting point of a major Brecht play that the author worked on intermittently for the next three years: *Saint Joan of the Stockyards.* Meanwhile there were three more important premières: *The Rise and Fall of the City of Mahagonny* (Leipzig, March 9, 1930), *The Measures Taken* (Berlin, December 10, 1930), and *The Mother* (Berlin, January 15, 1932).

It was especially the two last-named works that stamped Brecht as a communist, for in them he very forthrightly identified himself, not only with Marxist philosophy in general, but with the Communist Party in particular. It did not, of course, follow that the Party accepted the attentions of its enthusiastic wooer. This was, moreover, the era of Stalin's ascendancy in world communism: there was no friendliness in the movement toward any form of modernism in art. And style was not the only stumbling block. Party critics of *The Measures Taken* had grave reservations about its content. For, like other young converts, Brecht had a tendency to be "more royalist than the king."

How the tension between Brecht and the Party critics would have worked out will never be known. Hitler's rise to power (1932–1933) ended such luxuries. On January 28, 1933, a performance of *The Measures Taken* in Erfurt was broken up by the police, and proceedings for high treason were instituted. The burning of the Reichstag on February 27 precipitated a period of terror. Brecht had seen it coming, and slipped across the frontier with Helene Weigel on the following day. Their two children, Stefan and Barbara, were smuggled out later. After a few months in Switzerland, Brecht was enabled, by the well-to-do writer Karin Michaelis, to make his home in Denmark for the next six years. Black years for Europe, they were highly creative ones for Brecht. Compulsory withdrawal from politics left him all the more free to write. He completed a big play he had begun in Berlin, *Roundheads and Peakheads;* wrote *The Private Life of the Master Race, Mother Courage and Her Children, The Trial of Lucullus,* and *The Life of Galileo;* and began *The Good Woman of Setzuan.*

Hitler invaded Poland on September 1, 1939. Already in the summer of that year Brecht had considered Denmark too hot to hold him. The Nazi Embassy had long been harassing him there, and a Nazi invasion of Denmark was already talked of. He moved his family and collaborators to Stockholm, where the sculptress Nina Santesson made them welcome in her home on Lidingö island. When Sweden too feared a Nazi invasion, the Brecht "ensemble" moved on to Finland and the estate of another wealthy woman, Hella Wuolijoki. The play *Mister Puntila and His Man Matti* was originally written in collaboration with Wuolijoki, who, indeed, continued to regard herself as its coauthor to the end—possibly with justification. *The Resistible Rise of Arturo Ui* was written on Wuolijoki's estate in March 1941.

Marxist refugees from Hitler had gone off in various directions: some to fight in the Spanish War, some to live in the "Socialist Fatherland," a compact and rather important group to settle in Mexico City. It would not seem that Brecht seriously considered the first two possibilities—either one might easily have meant death—but he would probably have found his way to Mexico, had not one member of his entourage, Margarete Steffin, been refused entry. In May 1941, the whole group obtained visas to enter the U.S., and proceeded to cross the Soviet Union, but Miss Steffin never made it beyond Moscow, where she died of tuberculosis. On July 21 the group—Brecht, his wife, the two children, and Ruth Berlau, who was both his mistress and an invaluable collaborator—landed in San Pedro, California. This extended family soon settled down in a small frame house in Santa Monica.

Brecht was in America over six years, and seemed fully prepared to stay longer, yet he sank no real roots in American life. For one thing, America did not welcome his works. (As for the talents of Helene Weigel, a great actress, she was "used" in exactly one American film, for the space of about ten seconds, in a nonspeaking role.) But again, exclusion from social activities left Brecht free to write, and to the American years belong *The Visions of Simone Machard, Schweyk in World War II,* and, above all, *The Caucasian Chalk Circle.* He made strenuous efforts to get this last produced on Broadway, but there were to be no Broadway productions of Brecht plays till the sixties (and then only unsuccessful ones). The only productions Brecht had anything to do with while he was in America were a small Off-Broadway production of *The Private Life of the Master Race* (1945) and a limited run of *Galileo,* first in Hollywood, then at the Maxine Elliott Theater, New York (1947). But meanwhile, his works had begun to appear in print in America. The books led to college productions of the plays. And, after he had returned to Europe, an American audience for Brecht, located mostly in the universities, did grow up.

When *Galileo* opened at the Maxine Elliott on December 7, Brecht was already in Europe. There had taken place on October 30 a grotesque little tragicomedy, not on the stage of any theater, but on the floor of the Caucus Room of the Old House Office Building in Washington, D.C. Here Bertolt Brecht was cross-questioned by the House Committee on Un-American Activities. It was a case, as one wit put it, of the biologist being studied by the apes. Brecht found himself in this position, less because he was a "Hollywood writer" at a time when Hollywood was being combed for "conspirators" than because he was a friend of the Eisler brothers, one of whom, Gerhart, was an agent of the German and/or Russian Communist Party. And someone in American "security" suspected a connection between the Eislers and the J. Robert Oppenheimer case. (Since the Committee broadcast the hearings on the radio, the "Brecht program" could easily be recorded by any listener who possessed the right sound equipment, and today it can be heard on a Smithsonian/Folkways recording.)

Bertolt Brecht's next resting place was the upper floor of a pleasant, chalet-like Swiss house overlooking the lake of Zurich. From this spot (Feldmeilen) he tried to orient himself in a Europe that offered him various opportunities. One possibility was to buy a house in Salzburg and write for a much refurbished Salzburg Festival. With this in mind, he acquired Austrian citizenship—never relinquished. He was also in touch with Benno Frank, cultural officer of the U.S. Army in Germany, and it seems Frank would have placed Brecht back in his native Bavaria had the State Department not suddenly issued a warning against "promoting" communists. Frank then commended Brecht to the attention of the Russian cultural officer, Colonel Dymshitz. Dymshitz arranged for Brecht to be made welcome in East Berlin, where he spent his last half dozen years.

With historic and by now well-known results. On January 11, 1949, *Mother Courage* opened at the Deutsches Theater in East Berlin with Helene Weigel in the title role. Brecht and Erich Engel directed it with a "scratch" company of actors. At this point the Berlin Ensemble was just a group within the larger organization of the Deutsches Theater. Not till 1954 were they to have their own building, the Theater am Schiffbauerdamm (eventually the full title would be "Das Berliner Ensemble am Bertolt Brecht Platz"). But during the first years of the fifties, Brecht and Helene Weigel converted their group into the most impressive theatrical ensemble in the Western world. Possibly Brecht's writing suffered; but possibly, too, it was worth it. In any case he still did some writing: poems, theoretical prose, adaptations, and one full-length play, barely finished at his death, *Turandot*.

If people had raised political questions about Bertolt Brecht in 1932 and in 1947, they were obviously going to raise them during the fifties. His conduct on June 17, 1953, became a storm center of controversy, and has remained so. (Günter Grass came out with a play on the subject in 1965.) On that day, the workers of East Berlin rose in revolt against their government. Brecht wrote the Party chief, Walter Ulbricht, an expression of his loyalty. His letter to Ulbricht also contained some criticism of the regime, but Ulbricht struck it out when giving the letter to the press. One witness states that Brecht proposed to include more criticism in the letter, but that Käthe Rülicke, his friend and "secretary," persuaded him not to. Certainly he did not declare his solidarity with the rebels.

Nineteen fifty-six was another year of decision. The leader of the intracommunist revolt against Ulbricht, Wolfgang Harich, named Brecht as someone who was sympathetically close to his group. That was in October. But Brecht had died in August, and could not testify. His widow stuck by Ulbricht through thick and thin, and apparently would not have wished anyone to think her husband ever did otherwise.

Again, the main fact is that Brecht did *not* take a public stand against the East Berlin regime. On the contrary. He chose, finally, if for a mixture of reasons, to live in the East, and to give the regime some very solid support. His attacks, quite naturally, were on Western misdeeds. In January 1953, for example, he sent off telegrams to Albert Einstein, Ernest Hemingway, and Arthur Miller asking them to do something about Ethel and Julius Rosenberg. He was concerned with the threat to world peace presented, in his view, by the United States, and he was happy to receive (1954–1955) the Lenin Peace Prize (then still called the Stalin Peace Prize). Ironically, his acceptance speech, delivered in Moscow, was translated into Russian, at Brecht's request, by Boris Pasternak.

Brecht's life ended with some theatrical triumphs. In July 1954, the Berlin Ensemble played *Mother Courage* at the Théâtre des Nations in Paris, and in June 1955, played *The Caucasian Chalk Circle* under the same auspices. These prize-winning events laid the foundation of that international success which Brecht's work was to meet with all over Europe in the late fifties and throughout the sixties.

The Bertolt Brecht described by friends who saw him in his last year—the film director Erwin Leiser, the playwright Max Frisch—was a sick man. Knowing the trouble was with his heart, he said to Leiser: "At least one knows that death will be easy. One tap on the window and . . ." The tap came a little before midnight on August 14. One of the doctors who signed the autopsy was Müllereisert, a boyhood friend whose name is familiar to readers of *Manual of Piety*. Brecht lies buried today beneath the windows of his last home (Chausseestrasse 125) in the same cemetery as the remains of his second favorite philosopher, Hegel.

\*　\*　\*

Bertolt Brecht was nothing if not the creator of a new theater. New in all departments. Lighting, for instance. One of the first things the stranger notices in the Brecht theater in East Berlin is that the lighting is different. There are no gelatins on the lamps. All the light is "white." So a Brecht play has a different look even before we see *what* is on the stage. Costume, for instance. No one had ever seen a costume play that looked like *Mother Courage* or *Galileo*. Nor was the difference the accidental one of a guest designer or a special brainstorm. A view is taken of costumes that extends from one play to another. For one thing, they are not seen as costumes at all, but as clothes, which have been worn before. Or stage design. "This is neither naturalism nor any of the departures from naturalism that we know about," students say who have examined the stage created by Brecht's designers (chiefly, Caspar Neher and Teo Otto). These designers usually started from a bare stage and placed on it whatever objects the action of the play required. Art? The art is in (a) the design of each object and (b) the placing of the objects. Spectators were often surprised how drastic the logic was. For example: if the action, though set in a room, makes no use of walls, you present a room without walls. Not naturalism; but Brecht called it realism.

Sometimes the setting, instead of creating the mood (which in Brecht it never is supposed to do), is in direct contrast with the mood. Not a new idea in itself, but not an exhausted one either, and most people felt they *had* seen something new when they witnessed the interaction between setting and actor in the Pope scene of Galileo. Here there was the added piquancy that the setting is actually the costume. More precisely: what had been "setting"—the Pope's robe on a dummy—becomes costume as it is transferred to the Pope's body; and when he is fully dressed, it becomes "setting" again, because he is submerged under it.

Music, too, is used as comment, and therefore often in direct contrast to the moment and the word. In his book *Composing for the Films*, Hanns Eisler suggests that this should be a principle of movie music, replacing the present assumption, which is that music is mood music and always either reinforces or embellishes. Eisler composed his best music for Brecht, and his idea is an application of Brecht's most famous idea, *alienation* (*Verfremdung*).

*Fremd* is German for *alien*. Hegel and Marx had made a very important principle out of *Entfremdung*, the normal German word for alienation or estrangement. *Verfremdung* is Brecht's word for the process of *making* alien or strange. Now, since it is well known that *alienation,* especially in the writings of Karl Marx, is an appalling phenomenon—the estrangement of the worker from the ownership and meaning of what he works at—it will be asked: how can the Marxist Bertolt Brecht actually *call for* alienation?

But already in Hegel alienation is a positive as well as a negative thing. More important, perhaps, it is necessary. As Herbert Marcuse likes to put it, Hegel proved the power of negative thinking, proved, indeed, that thinking *is* negative by virtue of being analytic—it takes apart. Conversely, "positive thinking" blurs distinctions, dissolves meaning in a perhaps inspiring fog. In which fog we live our lives. To use a metaphor that brings us back to Brecht, we need to step *away* from a picture to come *closer* to seeing it.

In what Brecht called the bourgeois theater, an author's aim is to make the audience think: "This man is brilliant: he sees such things as I never saw." It was Brecht's ambition to make his audience say: "What this man shows me is no creation of his brilliance, it is the real world, which I realize I was out of touch with till he reminded me." This kind of "reminder," in Brecht's view, is not—is no longer—effected by naturalism. It requires the *alienation effect.* (Here the word "effect" [German: *Effekt*] also gives trouble. The right sense is suggested by our use of the plural, "effects.") In order that the buzz and blur of the circumambient world should become defined sound and image, the world itself has to be pushed away a little, even pushed to one side a little, and looked at askew—as Hogarth and Daumier knew. In this way, the world is "made alien" in order that it may be "made known." The logic is paradoxical, but what is involved is not a trickiness in reasoning, but complexity in the experience of discovery and realization. Colloquially, we say "I suddenly realized," but the suddenness comes at the end of a process, and the process does not resemble driving straight ahead on a highway. Rather, after a sharp turn left, immediately followed by a sharp turn right, one "suddenly realizes," *with a jolt,* that one is still moving ahead in the original direction. The jolt has defined the direction one is moving in for one's emotional system. It is an alienation effect.

Brecht often addressed himself to the topic of the A Effect (in German: *V-Effekt*) in acting, and it may well be that the most radical changes he demanded in the theater, other than in the writing, were in the acting.

"Three devices," he wrote, "can contribute to the alienation of the words and actions of the person presenting them: 1. the adoption of the third person, 2. the adoption of the past tense, and 3. the speaking of stage directions and comments." This meant that, in early rehearsals or class-room exercises, the dialogue of a scene should be translated from the first to the third person and from the present to the past tense and that an actor should read all stage directions aloud as they occur. A Brechtian playwright will sometimes even write scenes in the third person and the past tense, in which case no such translation is called for. A celebrated example is to be found in Brecht's own play *The Caucasian Chalk Circle*, and it will be noticed that the narration also includes what would normally be considered "stage directions and comments":

> *. . . And she rose, and bent down, and sighing,*
> *took the child*
> *And carried it off.*
> *As if it was stolen goods she picked it up.*
> *As if she was a thief she sneaked away.*

It is Brecht's thesis that if an actress will practice enacting such an incident while another performer reads the lines, she will eventually find she has acquired another *way* of acting, another *style,* the style of the new theater.

How does this differ from the style of the old theater? Precisely by alienating the narrative—and with it the character the actor is presenting. The difference has sometimes been understood thus: "In the pre-Brechtian theater, and notably in the Stanislavsky theater, the actor is completely identified with the character: he *is* the character, and *we* can completely identify ourselves with *him, we* are the character. In the Brechtian theater, on the other hand, the actor openly disowns the character, shows both himself *and* the character. By not identifying himself with the character, he prevents *us* from making the identification. Instead of losing ourselves in the character, we look at it from the outside." Which is correct but exaggerated. In no theater could there be *complete* identifications, or spectators would be rushing on stage to save the Desdemonas from the Othellos. In no theater could there be complete detachment, or the spectator would simply be excluded—and would detach himself from the whole occasion by going to sleep or walking out. A degree of identification is contained in the very idea of enactment. It is a question of what degree. And the whole difference of opinion on the matter represents a concern with *degree*. Brecht experimented to the end of finding out what *degree* of identification is needed and for what. If the aim is pathos, then you must make the identifications as nearly complete as theater art will permit, and this has been done in all the pathetic domestic dramas, from Victorian melodrama to radio soap opera, of the past hundred years. Conversely, if the aim were comedy, there would be nothing new (in that sense, nothing Brechtian) about resisting identifications. A traditional way of resisting identifications is for a comedian to break out of any role he may be playing and talk to the audience. If Brecht was an innovator in this area it was because he introduced this principle into dramaturgy itself: his characters often "break out" of a scene and address the audience. Generally, the songs, too, represent such a breakout, in contrast to the songs of the American "musical," which are made continuous with the dialogue.

Lighting, costume, stage design, music, acting, and, last but not least, playwriting itself: Brecht wanted to "make it new" in all these departments and took steps to do so both as writer and as stage director. One could even add directing to the list of departments, except that what it primarily means is the coordination of all the others. "Audience" is not, in this sense, a department, either. You wouldn't expect a section on "the people who eat" in a cookbook, and audience is not a category parallel to the theater arts themselves. On the other hand, just as cooking exists for eaters and no one else, so theater exists for spectators and no one else, and if a theater theoretician does not speak of them at *one* time it is because he has them in mind (in the back of his mind, perhaps) *all* the time. Every kind of theater represents a particular kind of operation performed upon the audience, and Brecht's originality consisted in his determination to perform a different operation on them.

What operation? In Brecht's pronouncements of the late twenties and early thirties, there is heavy emphasis on the didactic: the theater is to instruct. In his "Short Organum" (1948) the emphasis is shifted to pleasure: the theater must please. Brecht's shift in emphasis has sometimes been taken as a mellowing or even as simply a retreat to a more traditional position, as if his earlier preoccupation with teaching was later regarded as a waste of time. But this is to ignore much of what Brecht said in the later theoretical writings, as well as his later practice as a playwright. And the change of theory reflects a development in the practice.

13

It is the development from plays of the period 1928–1934, which he himself labeled didactic (*Lehrstücke*), such as *The Exception and the Rule,* to plays of the period 1938–1944, such as *Galileo, Mother Courage,* and *The Caucasian Chalk Circle.* And of these latter, it could be said that, while they are less didactic in form, they are more instructive in effect. Brecht's development was from a rather puritanic and perhaps even undialectical didacticism to a much fuller presentation of the dialectics of living. Correspondingly, he became dissatisfied with the name he gave his kind of work in the late twenties—Epic Theater—and at the end of his life was toying with the term Dialectical Theater.

There comes a point at which the distinction between pleasing and instructing does not help us anymore, for what Brecht wishes to do is not flatly either to please people or instruct them. It is something closer to waking them up. In the eighteenth century already, Schiller had complained that in the theater the Muse "takes to her broad bosom the dull-witted teacher and the tired businessman and lulls the spirit into a magnetic sleep by warming up the numbed senses and giving the imagination a gentle rocking." This describes just what the German theater was still doing in Brecht's youth, and while the older playwrights continued to purvey sleeping pills, the young Brecht manufactured an alarm clock.

The bedroom he planned to place it in was not that of the businessman. The positive emotional content of the new theater has to do with productivity, and corresponds to the joy of planners and builders. Indeed, in a society where the planning and building is rational, the worker on these tasks will find them reflected—jubilantly taken up in symbolic form—in the drama. The new theater will also have a negative emotional content. It will show impatience with whatever impedes the planning and building, anger at whatever opposes or wrecks it. These two bodies of emotional content will produce their own characteristic rhythm in the theater, will outcrop in plays which have a characteristic movement. First, there is the rhythm of joy, the movement toward fruition and achievement, best exemplified in Brecht's own work by *The Caucasian Chalk Circle.* Second, there is the rhythm of rage, the movement toward defiance and resistance, best exemplified by *Mother Courage.*

Anger and defiance were, of course, commonplaces of the social drama even before Brecht. But they seldom worked: that is to say, they only touched the surface. Millionaires could be roused to cry, "Strike!"

from their seats in the orchestra, but their zeal had subsided before they reentered their waiting limousines. What Brecht, on the other hand, says about anger in the scene devoted to the subject (*Mother Courage,* Scene 4) reveals what he has in mind for the theater. Getting worked up for an hour or two has no value. We need to generate enough anger to last a lifetime. Or rather, since we probably have that much already, we need to tap it, to make it available. This, as psychoanalysts know, can only be done by indirection. The indirections of Brechtian theater—its devices and "effects"—are ways of doing it. There could therefore be no greater error than to imagine that the purpose of Brecht was to exclude emotion. He sweeps aside facile tears because his concern is with deep passion, and he shares with religious thinkers the assumption that deep passion is seldom neutral but tends to be tied to convictions, to belong, as it were, either to God or the Devil. The Brechtian drama taps those deeper springs of feeling which, like the sentiment of faith as described by St. Paul (an allusion found in *Mother Courage,* Scene 4), can move mountains.

None of the innovations listed above (or any others that could be added) was to Brecht in the first instance an aesthetic matter. In that respect, he was not an "avant-garde" writer at all: none of his idiosyncrasies claim any interest in themselves. And even his later homage to pleasure brought with it no innovations that had the purveying of pleasure as their specific purpose. So what *is* he doing with his audience? It would be a fair summary of what has been reported here to state: he is helping the audience to *see* certain things and to *feel* certain things. But to this must now be added that the help is not extended because the "certain things" are interesting in themselves, let alone just because they are "there." It is extended because, in Dr. Samuel Johnson's words: "It is always the writer's duty to make the world better."

When, little more than a year before his death, Brecht was asked: "Can the world of today be represented on a stage?" he replied in the affirmative—"but only if it [the world] is regarded as transformable." For him, the stage is concerned with what men do to men and nothing else. And, unlike Jesus Christ, he believed that they do know what they do. They have chosen to do what they have done, and could choose otherwise. A description of their activities "makes no sense"—would have no point—if this were not true. Therefore even the most descriptive-seeming episode in a play must really be not descriptive at all, but normative. It implies either praise or blame. It moves history along, if only by a minute, invisible step, toward a different future. It is likely that, to Brecht, the most important statement in all history was this:

> The philosophers have only interpreted the world in various ways; the point, however, is to change it.

It is the eleventh thesis on Feuerbach of his favorite philosopher, Karl Marx.

# Comments on Three Brecht Plays

These are offered here as samples of Brecht criticism. If they are but one reader's (or spectator's) opinion, so much the better. As such they invite challenge and response from other readers: they initiate discussion. Brecht is nothing if not a controversial writer: let there be controversy.

Why these three plays? They represent three distinct aspects of Brecht: first, his supreme entertainment and contribution to musical theater; second, his celebrated form of didactic theater, raised here to tragic heights; and third, his grandest human drama and treatment of his ultimate theme: war.

## The Threepenny Opera

Lillian Hellman has said that the great plays of our time are *Threepenny Opera* and *Mother Courage*. I would add that a song named "The Solomon Song" is at the heart of both, and that they are really the same play.

"Vanity of vanity, saith the Preacher [i.e., Solomon], all is vanity," says the Bible, and its commentators explain that the reiterated word means emptiness, nullity: our life begins and ends in nothingness—a leitmotiv of literature, especially modern literature, especially Brecht and Beckett. "There is indeed no more to add: the world is poor and men are bad." There Mr. Peachum rests his case, and many have assumed that Brecht rested his there too.

Those who assume otherwise point to his Marxism, which in turn points to a world that is rich where men are good, and, to be sure, Marxism is either explicit or implicit or both in much of Brecht's later work. It is explicit in his *Notes to Threepenny Opera,* written later, as also in the new ending that was found for the *Threepenny Film* in 1930. *Threepenny*

*Opera* itself, though written only two years earlier, is another matter. Its politics do indeed seem to be summed up in the chorale at the end, as Marxist critics have not been slow to state:

> *Combat injustice, but in moderation:*
> *Such things will freeze to death if left alone.*
> *Remember: this whole vale of tribulation*
> *Is black as pitch and cold as any stone.*

Or, as Beckett would say: nothing to be done. It is true that the social relationships in the play depict the capitalist system, seen in a Marxist way, in miniature, but without the Marxist solution, without a rebellious and liberating proletariat. It is a kind of semi-Marxism, which only reinforces the sense of defeat inherent in the social order that Marxism seeks to replace.

One reason I call *Mother Courage* the same play as *Threepenny* is that it is imbued with the same sense of defeat. "The Solomon Song," sung in both plays, externally speaking comes as a digression in both plays, but is no digression thematically speaking:

> *King Solomon was very wise*
> *So what's his history?*
> *He came to view this world with scorn*
> *And curse the hour he was born*
> *Declaring all is vanity.*
> *King Solomon was very wise*
> *But long before the day was out*
> *The consequence was clear, alas,*
> *And wisdom 'twas that brought him to this pass:*
> *A man is better off without.*

In *Mother Courage,* the subject of the song is given as "the uselessness of the virtues." In *Threepenny,* there is a song called "The Futility of All Human Endeavor." In neither play is Marxist optimism invoked. I was present at a meeting of the Communist Youth (East Berlin, 1949) when the radical teenagers complained bitterly to Brecht himself of the pacifistic pessimism in *Mother Courage.* "An insult to our heroes fighting in wars of liberation all over the world," one boy said. Both *Mother Courage* and *Threepenny* dramatize class struggle, but in neither case is any development forward to a new synthesis, a higher stage of civilization, in any way affirmed.

But another kind of optimism is to be found in both plays—an optimism not grand and world-historical but apolitical, personal, temperamental, irrational, if you will, and yet not devoid of much clever, cynical rationality.

The premises of the Brechtian pessimism are a universe without God and a world without ethics. All heroic and saintly quests have become vain: the Holy Grail is not there, and our Don Quixotes are all Sancho Panzas. What room in this scheme of things for *any* positive element? Those who look in *Threepenny Opera* (and other early works of Brecht) for idealism will look in vain. The positive element is not idealistic but erotic and, as such, amoral. It would seem that even in the bleak climate of Brecht's early plays man cannot be discouraged from pleasure seeking—the pursuit of an orgasm to put it physiologically, the pursuit of happiness to put it philosophically. The only god that is known to have won Brecht's allegiance is a Chinese god of happiness which he encountered in the form of a statuette of a little fat man. And, as against Stalin, he was the god that didn't fail.

Clearly, the possibilities for happiness, even for pleasure, in that climate, are very circumscribed. "The wickedness of the world," says Peachum, "is so great you have to run your legs off to avoid having them stolen out from under you." Yet good times can be had if you are prepared to meet two conditions. The first is simply to recognize the narrow limits within which you must work: don't attempt to be more than a small-time hedonist—no paradises, no heavens, no Utopias, no Free Worlds. The second condition is willingness—also on a small scale—to be a crook, lie a little, steal a little, and keep your mouth shut at certain times. . . . I am outlining the philosophy of the woman Brecht called Courage. The play *Mother Courage* "explains" that, ultimately, this philosophy doesn't work. Non-ultimately, however, it did; and it was really a non-ultimate notion anyway.

It has often been remarked that, while *Mother Courage* is a very sad tale indeed, for about two thirds of the evening Brecht's audience is chuckling. There is a conclusion to draw here other than that Brecht was witty. It is that his character Mother Courage was having a good time, was as near to happy as mere human beings get: she had a lot of fun, she gave and took much good humor and warmth. Even in his somberest book of poems, *Manual of Piety,* Brecht could report:

> *Almost all men give thanks for their birth*
> *Before they receive their handful of earth.*

Still, philosophically, the emphasis, in *Mother Courage,* is on the negative, and Courage's willingness to accept small mercies and commit small offences is not recommended by the author. In this, the later play parts company with *Threepenny Opera,* for, as I see the earlier work, its final word, if it has one, is that in a big, bad world the best thing is to be a small, bad man. A good time is to be had, not, it is true, by all, but by those who meet the two conditions.

I know Mr. Peachum doesn't agree with me. At the end of *Threepenny Opera,* a reprieve comes by mounted messenger for the small, bad man—Mr. Macheath—who had been headed for the gallows, and Mr. Peachum says: "In reality [the] end is bad. Mounted messengers from the Queen come far too seldom, and if you kick a man he kicks you back again." It is a joke that goes all the way back to Brecht's source, *The Beggar's Opera* by John Gay (1728), where Macheath is reprieved because it's an opera and frivolous.

If there is a problem for critics in *Threepenny Opera,* it's in deciding what to take literally and what ironically. There is also such a thing in comedy as a double twist whereby irony is not accepted as such. Brecht duplicates Gay's ironical ending, but the irony is that he has removed the irony, and the point, in *Threepenny Opera,* is that a mounted messenger *has* come from the Queen, and it isn't the first time. Macheath—people like Macheath—bear a charmed life, are reprieved, and, having escaped from jail, if they are reimprisoned, escape again. And again. And again. If *Mother Courage* audiences chuckle, *Threepenny* audiences roar with laughter: quite provably, this is one of the great entertainments of the twentieth century, the show above all shows in which the repulsive debacle of modern history becomes delightful masquerade.

The dolce vita of Fellini's film was not *really* dolce. At the center of those good times was misery. Macheath, on the other hand, by a little crookedness earns himself a very good time indeed. If *Threepenny* is about capitalism, its conclusion is that, bad as the system is, and totally without historic prospects, you can have a good time in the holes and corners of it, the nooks and the crannies. No irony: this good time is good.

And here is the deeper reason why *Threepenny Opera* cannot express socialist optimism: it is too optimistic about capitalism. If in *The Good Woman of Setzuan* Brecht shows you can't be good under capitalism, in *Threepenny* he shows you can be happy under capitalism—if you're prepared to be bad. Granted, of course, that everything is relative, especially happiness, and you may not be very happy or happy for long.

It isn't just Mr. Peachum who disagrees with me. Mr. Brecht himself had quite different things to say in his *Notes*. But then he was inclined to change the meanings of his works after the fact. It was after the fact that he added lyrics to *Threepenny* in which the audience is warned against going after little crooks like Macheath while leaving at large crooks like the top Nazis. Brecht seems to have hoped that such inserts would successfully moralize this otherwise amoral work. Too late. Tagging on a few moralistic lines cannot change the temper and tone of a three-hour masterpiece. Besides, my point about Macheath is only reinforced by the later additions. Thus: until we have brought to heel the giant adventurers of big business and imperialism, there is no reason not to tolerate the dwarf adventurers of small business and "highway robbery." Mother Courage says: "We're prisoners. But so are lice in fur." Macheath is a prisoner of a certain economic system. That's the fur; he is definitely a louse.

"The Solomon Song," vehicle of the ostensible pessimism of *Threepenny Opera,* has this to say:

*And here you see our friend Macheath:*
*His life is now at stake.*
*So long as he was rational*
*And took whate'er there was to take*
*His fame was international.*
*But then he got emotional*
*And though the day is not yet out*
*The consequence is clear, alas!*
*Emotion 'twas that brought him to this pass:*
*A man is better off without.*

"This pass" is mortal danger. Macheath is about to be placed in the death cell. He will be saved from death only by an intervention which, Peachum says, wouldn't happen in real life. But Peachum is not Brecht. And later Brecht is not the Brecht who wrote *Threepenny Opera.* And early Brecht believed life could be good while it lasted. "Emotion" (Eros) was not fatal to Macheath, or not immediately so, and nothing in any case lasts forever.

If Macheath does not embody saintliness or heroism or any idea of virtue, he does embody Eros, the Life Force. In other respects the most negative of "heroes," he is in this respect decisively positive. Brecht's *Notes* say No: they have it that it is not passion that drives Macheath to the whorehouse each Thursday, and thus enables the Peachums to plan his capture on a Thursday: it is the bourgeois sense of order, dictating that what is done on many Thursdays must be done on all. This is a joke *made only in the Notes.* In the original story, Macheath is obviously driven by lust like Brecht's other early "heroes," especially Baal, whose reincarnation Macheath is. One of the lyrics speaks of his "sexual submissiveness," but that *is* simple irony—the singer is Mrs. Peachum—and Macheath "submits" to sex, just as Baal does, with delicious, self-indulging passivity. The Chinese god of pleasure, Baal, and Macheath are all one.

In a late work of Brecht's, next to a picture of the Chinese god, these words are printed: "happiness, that is, communism." *Threepenny Opera* dates back to a time when Brecht had not yet really "found" the positive part of communism and so happiness was officially nowhere. Unofficially, I have suggested, it subsisted in nooks and crannies. A Marxist might put it that this happiness was to be found specifically in the petty bourgeoisie and Lumpenproletariat, themselves nooks and crannies between bourgeoisie and proletariat. He might add that, later, Macheath would have to choose between being forced down into the proletariat or taking a job as a guard in a concentration camp.

Behind the whole story lies one of the supreme comic masters of all time, Jonathan Swift, for it was he who gave Gay the idea for *The Beggar's Opera.* The image Swift created was that of a "Newgate pastoral." Pastoral literature portrayed a golden age of love and perpetual youth: conflict and death were simply wished away. Swift saw comic, satiric possibilities in equating this unreal other world with the ultrareal world of jailbirds and whores. An exquisite irony! And again we find Bertolt Brecht doing some further ironizing on his own. More important, we again find him taking away much of the preexistent irony, for the point he would above all make is that, in the interstices, the cracks, of our prosaic, life-hating society, a certain degree of "pastoral poetry" (death-defying erotic fun) remains "quite a thought," even a real possibility. *Threepenny* is even more of a Newgate pastoral than *The Beggar's Opera*.

## The Measures Taken

*It is utter folly to be wise all by yourself.*
—LA ROCHEFOUCAULD

1977. The government of the U.S.A. would like the government of the U.S.S.R. to respect "human rights."

Sarcastic commentators have not been slow to point out that the rights implied—notably, *habeas corpus*—are not held by the citizenry of most countries in the world—are not held, even, by most of the countries designated "friendly" to the U.S.A. One of the "friendliest," Iran, is indeed one of the most unfriendly to those rights and to all individual freedoms.

That, we say, is politics, and we think perhaps of Brendan Behan's remark: "I'll never make a politician, I've only got one face." If we are cynics, we leave the matter there: "rights" are something that belong to ideology and propaganda; in practice they can be, and are, discounted. We all preach rights; we just don't practice what we preach.

One thing wrong with cynicism in this case is that it overlooks the fact that many honorable and intelligent persons have not preached—have not believed in—such rights. One of these persons is the father of Western philosophy, Plato, who, in *The Laws* 942AB, wrote:

> The principal thing is that none, man or woman, should ever be without an officer set over him, and that none should get the mental habit of taking any step, whether in earnest or in jest, on his individual responsibility: in peace as in war he must live always with his eye on his superior officer, following his lead and guided by him

in his smallest actions. . . . In a word, we must train the mind not even to consider acting as an individual or know how to do it.

This is Plato in what is sometimes called his Spartan vein, and there is a clue in the word Spartan, in that what distinguished Sparta was the subordination of all other elements in its culture to the military factors.

There can be little doubt that the chief model of social order throughout Western history has been the military model, and of this proposition the converse is that whenever a regime has made order its highest priority it has by that token proclaimed the military state. Prussia is a famous example, and in the Articles of War of the Prussian Army in the time of the author of *The Prince of Homburg* and *The Marquise of O.* we read that a Prussian officer must obey his superior "even against his own honor." And if this strikes you as a peculiarly Prussian extremism, remind yourself that the founder of the Society of Jesus had laid it down that, faced with a conflict between individual conscience and obedience to the Order, the Jesuit must commit himself to obedience. Ignatius Loyola had transferred the military discipline of his soldiering youth to a religious Order—an idea of genius, perhaps, but hardly an idea of liberty.

It is, of course, only in countries where the citizens have won those individual rights that there is any broad contrast between military and civilian law. In such countries, civilians may well be shocked by Bertolt Brecht's *Measures Taken* because of its clear-cut defense of the right of the group to liquidate the individual in the group interest. Even they, however, would probably not be shocked if the story were placed in a wartime setting. Noncivilians could hardly be shocked (unless they are also stupid) since no general could run a battle except on the assumptions about solidarity and obedience that are made by Brecht in his play. Ethics aside, the practicalities of strategy and tactics require that when a decision is taken by the High Command it be carried out by the soldiery.

But our Western audiences have three more reasons for being shocked at *The Measures Taken:* (1) that, as they see it, the situation depicted is not a wartime situation; (2) that the disciplinarians are communists, who we have been brought up to believe are our mortal foes; and (3) that the individual sacrificed is not a traitor, malingerer, or fool but the "good guy" of the outfit, apparently getting his for his very goodness.

The first two of these three reasons are at bottom the same, for Karl Marx proposed to regard the struggle between the peoples and world capitalism as a war, a universal civil war—the class war. The only ethics, therefore, would be, in a clear sense, military ethics. "We derive our morality," Lenin put it, "from the interests of the proletarian class war."

And the third reason for being shocked at *The Measures Taken* is particularly poignant since, for the Western spectator, that good guy, punished for his very goodness, is himself. For obviously every spectator who is not a communist and therefore does not identify himself with the Party when he sees this play, identifies himself with the Young Comrade—except, no doubt, when the latter identifies *himself* with the Party and agrees to his own execution.

Now it is a well-known part of the Brechtian theory that we must not identify ourselves with the protagonist, at any rate not to the extent we have expected to. In the light of this principle it was quite cunning of Brecht to permit us an identification with the Young Comrade, then, suddenly, to shock us out of that identification. At this point, indeed, we withdraw angrily from our entanglement in history with the word *No!* on our lips.

Well, such is dialectical drama. Brecht suggests, in a note, that if you wish to learn something more after playing the part of the Young Comrade, you should play one of the Agitators; after which you should try singing in the Control Chorus; switching roles in a political psychodrama in order to get the feel of the other standpoint.

And dialectics works both ways. An actor who had sung in the Chorus or played an Agitator would have it borne quite strongly in on him, when he then played the Young Comrade, to what extent Brecht wrote sympathy into that role, gave it a certain dignity, brought it to the verge (though not over the verge) of pathos.

*And we looked and in the twilight saw*
*His naked face, human, open, guileless . . .*

In the New Testament, there is a story of a zealous young man who thought he could win the Authorities over to his view of things. He was wrong. They put him to death. Yet "all that sat in the Council, looking steadfastly upon him, saw his face, as it had been the face of an angel." The New Testament tells the story from the young man's viewpoint: he is Stephen, the first Christian martyr. And it is interesting that Communist Party critics, back in 1930, wished Brecht had taken Stephen's—the Young Comrade's—side, just as his "bourgeois" readers and spectators still do. A nondialectical drama, one concludes, would have suited everybody, while very likely boring everybody too. *The Measures Taken,* as we have it, suits nobody. But it also bores nobody and, I venture to think, has something in it for everybody.


## Mother Courage

Mother Courage *clambered onto the English-speaking stage rather clumsily. In Britain, Joan Littlewood, Eithne Dunne, and Flora Robson all tried the part early on. Beatrice Manley was the first American Courage at the Actors' Workshop, San Francisco, 1955. Jerome Robbins directed the play on Broadway in 1963 with a cast that included Anne Bancroft, Gene Wilder, Mike Kellin, Zohra Lampert, and Barbara Harris. The following piece was written for the National Theatre's production, London, 1965.*

The role of Mother Courage is hard to play and is always being miscast. Why? "Because middle-aged actresses are such ladies and lack earthiness." But who has succeeded in the role? Outstandingly, Helene Weigel. Is she very earthy, is she notably proletarian? On the contrary—there is nothing proletarian about her except her opinions. Then what is it those other women lack that Helene Weigel has? Among other things, an appreciation of the role, an understanding of what is in it, and above all the ability to portray contradictions. For whenever anyone says, "Mother Courage is essentially X," it is equally reasonable for someone to retort: "Mother Courage is essentially the opposite of X."

*Mother Courage is essentially courageous.* That is well known, isn't it? Tennessee Williams has written of the final moment of Brecht's play as one of the inspiring moments in all theater—inspiring because of the woman's indomitability. On she marches with her wagon after all that has happened, a symbol of the way humanity itself goes on its way after all that has happened, *if* it can find the courage. And after all we don't have to wait for the final scene to learn that we have to deal with a woman of considerable toughness and resilience. This is not the first time she has shown that she can pick up the pieces and continue. One might even find courage in the very first scene, where we learn that she has not been content to cower in some corner of Bamberg but has boldly come to meet the war. A troublemaker, we might say on first meeting the lady, but the reverse of a coward.

Yet it is impossible to continue on this tack for long without requiring an *on the other hand.* Beginning with the reason why she is nicknamed "Courage" in the first place.

> They call me Mother Courage because I was afraid I'd be ruined, so I drove through the bombardment of Riga like a madwoman with fifty loaves of bread in my cart. They were going moldy, what else could I do?

Did those who gave her the name intend a joke against an obvious coward? Or did they think she was driven by heroic valor when in fact she was impelled by sheer necessity? Either way her act is utterly devoid of the moral quality imputed. Whether in cowardice or in down-to-earth realism, her stance is Falstaffian. What is courage? A word.

Somewhere hovering over this play is the image of a preeminently courageous mother who courageously tries to hold on to her young. More than one actress, offering herself for the role, has seen this image and nothing else. Yet valor is conspicuously absent at those times when Mother Courage (however unwittingly) seals the fate of her children. At moments when, in heroic melodrama, the protagonist would be riding to the rescue, come hell or high water, Mother Courage is in the back room concluding a little deal. For her, it is emphatically not "a time for greatness." *She is essentially cowardly.*

A basic contradiction, then, which the actress in the role must play both sides of, or the play will become the flat and simple thing which not a few journalistic commentators have declared it to be. An actress may be said to be beginning to play Mother Courage when she is putting both courage and cowardice into the role with equal conviction and equal effect. She is still only beginning to play it, though; for, as she proceeds with her interpretation, she will find that, in this play, courage and cowardice are not inherent and invariable qualities but by-products.

Of what? We can hunt for the answer by looking further into particular sequences of action. It is not really from cowardice that Mother Courage is in the back room concluding a little deal when her children are claimed by the war. It is from preoccupation with "business." Although *Mother Courage* is spoken of as a war play, it is actually a business play, in the sense that the incidents in it, one and all, are business transactions—from the deal with the belt in Scene One, through the deal with the capon in Scene Two, the deal with the wagon in Scene Three, the deals with bullets and shirts in Scene Five, through to the economical funeral arrangements of the final scene. And since these transactions (except for the last) are what Courage supports her children by, they are "necessary." Those who condemn her have to face the question: What alternative had she? Of what use would it have been to save the life of Swiss Cheese if she lacked the wherewithal to *keep* him alive? The severe judge will answer that she could take a chance on this, provided she does save his life. But this is exactly Mother Courage's own position. She is fully prepared to take the chance if she has to. It is in determining whether she has to that her boy's life slips through her fingers: life or death is a matter of timing.

To say that Swiss Cheese is a victim of circumstances, not of Courage's character, will not, however, be of much use to the actress interpreting this character. If cowardice is *less* important here than at first appears, what is *more* important? Surely it is a failure in understanding, rather than in virtue. Let me elaborate.

Though only one of Brecht's completed plays is about anyone that a university would recognize as a philosopher, several of his plays present what one might call philosophers in disguise, such as Schweyk, the philosopher of a pub in Prague, and Azdak, the philosopher of a Georgian village. To my mind, *Mother Courage is above all a philosopher,* defining the philosopher along Socratic lines as a person who likes to talk all the time and explain everything to everybody. (A simple trait in itself, one would think, yet there have been actresses and directors who wish to have all Courage's speeches shortened into mere remarks. Your philosopher never makes remarks; he always speechifies; such abridgment enforces a radical misinterpretation of character.) I do not mean at all that Courage is an idle or armchair philosopher whose teachings make no contact with life. On the contrary, her ideas are nothing if not a scheme of life by which, she hopes, her family is to do pretty well in a world which is doing pretty badly.

Here one sees the danger of thinking of Mother Courage as the average person. Rather, she resembles the thoughtfully ambitious modern mother of the lower-middle or better-paid working class who wants her children to win scholarships and end up in the Labour Cabinet. (Minister of Education: Kattrin. Chancellor of the Exchequer: Swiss Cheese. Minister of War: Eilif.) Has it escaped attention that if one of her children turns out a cutthroat, this is blamed on circumstances ("Otherwise, I'd have starved, smarty"), while *the other two are outright heroes?* Anyone who considers this an average family takes a far higher view of the average than is implicit in the works of Bertolt Brecht.

What is the philosophy of this philosopher? Reduced to a single proposition, it is that if you concede defeat on the larger issue, you can achieve some nice victories in smaller ways. The larger issue is whether the world can be changed. It can't. But brandy is still drunk and can be sold. One can survive, and one can help one's children to survive by teaching each to make appropriate use of the qualities God gave him. The proposition I have just mentioned will apply to this upbringing. A child endowed with a particular talent or virtue should not pursue it to its logical end: defeat on such projects should be conceded at the outset. The child should cunningly exploit his characteristic talent for its incidental uses along the way. In this fashion the unselfishness of a Swiss Cheese or a Kattrin can be harnessed to selfishness. The result, if the philosophy works, is that while the world may shoot itself to blazes, the little Courage family, one and all, will live out its days in moderate wealth and moderate happiness. The scheme is not utopian. Just the opposite: the hope is to make optimism rational by reducing human demands to size.

The main reason it doesn't work is that the little world which Mother Courage's wisdom tries to regulate is dependent upon the big world which she has given up as a bad job. Small business is part of the big war which is part of the big business of ownership of *all* the means of production and distribution. No more than the small businessman can live in a separate economic system from the big can the small philosopher live in a separate philosophic system from the big. *Mother Courage,* one can conclude, exposes the perennial illusions of the *petit bourgeois* scheme of things. This has often been done before in modern literature. But usually only the idealism has been exposed. Mother Courage, on the other hand, could claim to be a cynic. She has the theater audience laughing most of the time on the score of this cynicism—by which *she* deflates illusions. Cynicism is nothing, after all, if not "realistic." What a cynical remark lays bare *has* to be the truth. Brecht makes the truth of his play the more poignant through the fact that the cynicism in it ultimately favors illusion. Mother Courage had gone to all lengths to trim her sails to the wind but even then the ship wouldn't move. So there is irony within irony (as, in Brecht's work, there usually is). Courage's cynicism can cut down the windy moralizing of the Chaplain easily enough, but only to be itself cut down by a world that cannot be comprehended even by this drastically skeptical thinking.

What alternative did Mother Courage have? The only alternatives shown in the play are, on the one hand, the total brutalization of men like the Swedish Commander (and, for that matter, her own son Eilif) and, on the other hand, the martyrdom achieved by Swiss Cheese and Kattrin. Presumably, to the degree that the playwright criticizes her, he is pushing her toward the second alternative. Yet, not only would such a destiny be out of character, within the terms of the play itself it is not shown to be preferable. Rather, the fruitlessness of both deaths is underlined. Why add a third?

Given her character, Mother Courage had no alternative to what she thought—or, for that matter, to the various "bad" things she did. In this case, can she be condemned? Logically, obviously not; but was Brecht logical? The printed editions of the play indicate that he made changes in his script to render Mother Courage less sympathetic. After having made her thoroughly sympathetic in his first version, Brecht later wanted her less so. One can see the sense of the changes in polemical terms: he did not wish to seem to condone behavior which is to be deplored. But to make this point, is it necessary to make Mother Courage a less good person? Personally I would think not, and I should like to see *Courage* played sometime in the Urtext of 1940 and without the later "improvements." But one should not minimize the complexity of the problem. Like many other playwrights, Brecht wanted to show a kind of inevitability combined with a degree of free will, and if it doesn't matter whether Courage is less good or more, because she is trapped by circumstances, then the play is fatalistic. I tend to think it *is* fatalistic as far as the movement of history is concerned, and that the element of hope in it springs only from Brecht's rendering of human character. Brecht himself is not satisfied with this and made changes in the hope of suggesting that things might have been different had Mother Courage acted otherwise. (What would she have done? Established socialism in seventeenth-century Germany?)

Brecht has stressed, in his Notes, that Mother Courage never sees the light, never realizes what has happened, is incapable of learning. As usual, Brecht's opinions, as stated in outside comments, are more doctrinaire than those to be found embodied in the plays. It may be true that Mother Courage never sees that "small business" is a hopeless case, though to prove even this Brecht had to manufacture the evidence by inserting, later, the line at the end: "I must get back into business." She does see through her own philosophy of education. The "Song of Solomon" in Scene Nine concedes that the program announced in Scene One has failed. The manipulation of the virtues has not worked: "a man is better off without." The song is more symbolic, as well as more schematic, than most Brechtians wish Brecht to be, for there is a verse about each of her children under the form of famous men (Eilif is Caesar, Swiss Cheese is Socrates, Kattrin is Saint Martin), but more important is that this is the "Song of Solomon" (from *The Threepenny Opera*) and that Solomon is Courage herself:

> *King Solomon was very wise*
> *So what's his history?*
> *He came to view this world with scorn*
> *Yes, he came to regret he ever had been born*
> *Declaring: all is vanity.*
> *King Solomon was very wise*
> *But long before the day was out*
> *The consequence was clear, alas:*
> *It was his wisdom brought him to this pass.*
> *A man is better off without.*

I have heard the question asked whether this conclusion was not already reached in the "Song of the Great Capitulation" in Scene Four. Both songs are songs of defeat (Brecht's great subject) but of two different defeats. The second is defeat total and final: Courage has staked everything on wisdom, and wisdom has ruined her and her family. The first is the setback of "capitulation," that is: of disenchantment. When Yvette was only seventeen she was in love, and love was heaven. Soon afterward she had learned to "fraternize behind the trees": she had capitulated. It is perhaps hard to imagine Courage as a younger and different person from the woman we meet in the play, but in the "Song of the Great Capitulation" we are definitely invited to imagine her as a young woman who thought she could storm the heavens, whose faith seemed able to move mountains.

Scene Four is one of several in this play which one can regard as the whole play in miniature. For Brecht is not finished when he has set forth the character of Mother Courage as one who has passed from youthful idealism to cynical realism. For many a playwright, that would no doubt be that, but Courage's exchange with the angry young soldier leads to other things. We discover that Mother Courage is not a happy Machiavellian, boasting of her realism. She is deeply ashamed. We discover in Courage the mother of those two roaring idealists (not to say again: martyrs) Swiss Cheese and Kattrin. "Kiss my ass," says the soldier, and why? His bad language had not hitherto been directed at her. But she has been kind to him only to be cruel. If she has not broken his spirit, she has done something equally galling: she has made clear to him how easily his spirit can be broken. When you convert a man to the philosophy of You Can't Win, you can hardly expect to earn his gratitude at the same time.

In the way Courage puts matters to the soldier we see how close she came to being a truly wise woman. We also discover in this scene that, despite the confident tone of her cynical lingo, Courage is not really sure of herself and her little philosophy. She teaches the soldier that it is futile to protest, but she apparently does not know this until she reminds herself of it, for she has come here to protest. Here we learn to recognize in Courage not only contradiction but conflict. She knows what she has thought. She is not sure what to think.

And this is communicated by Brecht in a very bold—or just poetic—manner. For while Courage does not give herself to despair until the end (and not even then for those who can take at face value her: "I must get back into business"), she had correctly foreseen the end from the beginning: the despair she gives herself to had been there from the moment of capitulation. At times it would strike her between the eyes: she is very responsive and has worked out the Marxist interpretation of religion for herself. Scene Two contains a song she had taught Eilif as a boy: it predicts the manner of his death. In Scene One she predicts doom for the whole family in her pantomime of fortune-telling. It could be said that everything is there from the start, for the first thing Mother Courage does is to try and sell things by announcing an early death for her prospective customers. The famous "Song of Mother Courage" is the most extraordinary parody of the kind of song any real *vivandière* might try to attract customers with. Mother Courage's "Come and buy!" is nothing other than: "Come and die!" In that respect, her fortune-telling is on the level, and her wisdom is valid.

Scene Four, I have been saying, is one of several in this play which one can regard as the whole play in miniature. The main purpose of the play, for Brecht, was, I think, to generate anger over what it shows. Yet Brecht realizes how pointless angry plays have been—and angry speeches outside the drama. It is said that Clifford Odets's *Waiting for Lefty* made millionaires angry for as long as it took them to get from their seats to where their chauffeurs tactfully waited for them at the end of the block. Such is the anger of the social drama in general.

There is the anger of a sudden fit, which boils up and over and is gone. And there is the anger which informs the work of long years of change. *Why* can't the world be changed? For Mother Courage, it is not from any inherent unchangeability in the world. It is because our wish to change it is not strong enough. Nor is this weakness innate. It is simply that our objection to the present world isn't as strong as it once was. What is outrageous does not outrage us as it once did. It only arouses the "short rage" of Brecht's soldier—and of Courage herself—not the long one that is required. Because we—they—have capitulated.

Capitulation is not an idea but a feeling, an agony, and is located not just in the scene of the Great Capitulation but in the whole play of *Mother Courage.* Everything that happens is related to it, above all the things that are furthest away from it: the deaths of Swiss Cheese and Kattrin. If these children are what their mother made them, then their refusal to capitulate stems from her, is her own youth, her own original nature.

The ultimate achievement of an actress playing this role would be that she made us sense to what an extent Courage's children are truly hers.

# A Guide to Reading, Listening, and Viewing

There follow here several lists and some words of advice. With the titles of books are given the names of publishers and at least the date of first publication. No publishers' names are provided with the titles of the plays, however, since in the United States there is no collected works from a single publisher, nor yet a set of the complete plays. Brecht has had many publishers in the U.S., and a glance at *Books in Print* will reveal that he has a number of different American publishers at any given time. This study guide is published by Grove Press, which at one time had fourteen volumes of Brecht in print and currently has nine. Grove is also the publisher of Eric Bentley's *Brecht Commentaries* and John Fuegi's *Brecht and Company*.

## Plays

*Baal,* 1918
*Trommeln in der Nacht* (Drums in the Night), 1918–20
*Im Dickicht der Städte* (In the Jungle of the Cities), 1921–23
*Mann ist Mann* (A Man's a Man), 1924–25
*Die Dreigroschenoper* (The Threepenny Opera), 1928
*Aufstieg und Fall der Stadt Mahagonny* (Rise and Fall of the City of
    Mahagonny), 1928–29
*Das Badener Lehrstück vom Einverständnis* (The Didactic Play of Baden:
    On Consent), 1928–29
*Die heilige Johanna der Schlachthöfe* (St. Joan of the Stockyards),
    1929–30
*Die Massnahme* (The Measures Taken), 1930
*Die Mutter* (The Mother), 1930–32
*Furcht und Elend des dritten Reiches* (Fear and Misery in the Third
    Reich), 1935–38

*Mutter Courage und ihre Kinder* (Mother Courage and Her Children), 1939
*Das Verhör des Lukullus* (The Trial of Lucullus), 1939
*Leben des Galilei* (Galileo), 1938–40
*Der gute Mensch von Sezuan* (The Good Woman of Setzuan), 1938–40
*Herr Puntila und sein Knecht Matti* (Mr. Puntila and His Man, Matti), 1940–41
*Der aufhaltsame Aufstieg des Arturo Ui* (The Resistible Rise of Arturo Ui), 1941
*Schweyk im zweiten Weltkrieg* (Schweik in the Second World War), 1941–44
*Die Gesichte der Simone Machard* (The Visions of Simone Machard), 1941–44
*Der kaukakische Kreidekreis* (The Caucasian Chalk Circle), 1944–45
*Antigone,* 1947
*Die Tage der Kommune* (Days of the Commune), 1948–49
*Der Hofmeister* (The Tutor), 1950
*Turandot,* 1953–54, unfinished

## Translated Poems and Songs in Book Form

*Selected Poems.* Translated by H. R. Hays. New York: Reynal and Hitchcock, 1947.
*Manual of Piety.* Translated by Eric Bentley. New York: Grove Press, 1966.
*The Brecht-Eisler Song Book.* Edited and with translations by Eric Bentley. New York: Oak Publications, 1967 (later taken over by Music Sales Corporation, New York).
*Poems 1913–1956.* Edited by John Willett and Ralph Manheim. London and New York: Methuen, 1976.

## Biography and Criticism

In the years since his death in 1956, dozens of volumes, in many languages, have been published on Brecht. The following list of seventeen ʒmits itself to English-language publications, but if it purports to offer venteen best, that is only the opinion of the writer of this guide (and since his own name is at the head of the list he can at once be suspected of bias). But here goes: *The Playwright as Thinker* was the book in which many American and British readers first heard about Brecht and his importance to modern theater. Later Eric Bentley wrote a memoir about his own direct relationship with Brecht and a book of commentaries on Brecht's plays as, over the years, they had come to his attention (he was the editor of the Grove Press editions of the playwright's works). Among the seventeen titles below, three are biographies of Brecht, and one contains a mini-biography. The pioneer work among these three is Klaus Völker's 1975 opus (translated from the German). Hayman's is the British biography, and Fuegi's *Brecht and Company* the American one. Fuegi's book may be said to replace the other two in that it restates their facts and adds many, many others. It must therefore be called a necessary book in the field, even though some of its conclusions are highly controversial and may not be widely accepted. As a Brecht authority, Fuegi has a rival in John Willett, one of whose books on Brecht is cited here. On the subject of Brecht in America (where he lived from 1941 to 1947), there is James Lyon's book and a lengthy section of Fuegi's *Brecht and Company*. The book that contains the mini-biography is Martin Esslin's breakthrough book of 1960, *Brecht: The Man and His Work*. Erika Munk's volume can be a good introduction to Brecht as it contains both significant excerpts from his hard-to-find works and some representative opinions of critics and scholars. Peter Demetz had collected such opinions ten years earlier. Munk and Demetz together introduce the reader to some two dozen commentators on the *Meister*.

It would be pointless to state which of the items below are in print: the answer will not be the same when readers encounter this study guide as it was when it went to press. But it is a safe guess that some of these items will have to be sought in libraries rather than bookstores. Dates provided here are those of first editions only.

Bentley, Eric. *The Playwright as Thinker*. New York: Reynal and Hitchcock, 1946.
———. *The Brecht Commentaries*. New York: Grove Press; London: Eyre Methuen, 1981.
———. *The Brecht Memoir*. New York: PAJ Publications, 1985.
Demetz, Peter, ed. *Brecht: A Collection of Critical Essays*. Englewood Cliffs, N.J.: Prentice-Hall, 1962.

Dickson, Keith A. *Towards Utopia: A Study of Brecht.* Oxford: Claren-
don, 1978.

Esslin, Martin. *Brecht: The Man and His Work.* Garden City, N.Y.:
Doubleday Anchor, 1960.

Fuegi, John. *Bertolt Brecht: Chaos According to Plan.* Cambridge: Cambridge University Press, 1987.

————. *Brecht and Company.* New York: Grove Press, 1994.

Hayman, Ronald. *Brecht: A Biography.* New York: Oxford University
Press, 1983.

Lyon, James K. *Bertolt Brecht in America.* Princeton, N.J.: Princeton
University Press, 1980.

Munk, Erika, ed. *Brecht.* New York: Bantam Books, 1972.

Spalter, Max. *Brecht's Tradition.* Baltimore, Md.: Johns Hopkins Press,
1967.

Völker, Klaus. *Brecht Chronicle.* Trans. Fred Wieck. New York: The
Seabury Press, 1975.

————. *Brecht: A Biography.* Trans. John Nowell. New York: The Seabury Press, 1978.

White, Alfred D. *Bertolt Brecht's Great Plays.* London: Macmillan; New
York: Harper & Row, 1978.

Willett, John. *The Theatre of Bertolt Brecht.* Norfolk, Conn.: New Directions, 1959.

Witt, Hubert, ed. *Brecht as They Knew Him.* Trans. John Peet. New
York: International Publishers, 1974.

## Audio and Video Recordings

A comprehensive account of Brecht on film, videotape, records, cassette
tapes, and compact discs would fill a far larger volume than this guide.
Offered here is just a word of advice in the field.

Teachers should certainly use such material as a teaching aid not
only in the classroom but also for home listening and viewing. Probably a
lot of it is already to be found in the nearest university library and easily
located either under Brecht's name or under the name of the composer—
above all, Kurt Weill. The four film versions of *The Threepenny Opera*
starring Rudolf Foerster [1931], Albert Préjean [1931], Kurt Jurgens
1965], and Raul Julia [1987]) have all (except for the Préjean) been popu-

lar enough in the early 1990s to be found in video rental stores. Sometimes, when a work has been on TV, although it is not commercially available on videotape, it will have been taped for a university theater or music department. (An example is *Mahagonny* as produced at New York's Metropolitan Opera.) As regards audio recordings, the best cue is often the name of a soloist, such as Lotte Lenya, who recorded in the thirties, forties, and fifties, or Ute Lemper, who is recording in the nineties.

Appended here is a list of records (now cassette tapes) made by or for the author of this study guide:

*Bentley on Brecht: A Bertolt Brecht Miscellany.* Performed by Eric Bentley. Folkways,* FH 5434.

*Brecht Before the Un-American Activities Committee.* A recording of the hearing. Folkways, FD 5531.

*The Elephant Calf.* The National Company cast album. Folkways, FL 9831.

*The Exception and the Rule.* The Off-Broadway cast album with Joseph Chaikin. Folkways, FL 9849.

*A Man's a Man.* The Off-Broadway cast album. Spoken Arts,* SA 870.

*Songs of Hanns Eisler.* Most of them to words by Brecht. Folkways, FH 5433.

*Both Folkways and Spoken Arts are today parts of larger entities. Folkways has been taken over by the Smithsonian Institution in Washington, D.C., and Spoken Arts was sold in 1990 to SBF Services, Inc., of Pinellas Park, Florida.

# About the Author of This Guide

Eric Bentley, one of the foremost authorities on the modern theater and a longtime intimate of Bertolt Brecht's, both personally and professionally, is the author of *The Brecht Commentaries* and *The Brecht Memoir*. Bentley has translated and edited most of Brecht's major works and has written introductions and forewords to many of these volumes, in which he examines with great acuity the complex layers of movement and meaning in Brecht's work. Rolf Fjelde has said that "the Eric Bentley versions of Brecht, in thought and feeling, language and theatricality, have proved themselves again and again ideally suited to convey the power of the originals to American audiences." Eric Bentley was born in England in 1916; he is a critic, playwright, director, performer, and teacher; his works include *The Life of the Drama* and *The Kleist Variations*.

# Ordering Information

Grove/Atlantic, Inc. (Grove Press and Atlantic Monthly Press) titles are available from Grove/Atlantic, Inc.'s distributor, Publishers Group West.

For customer service inquiries or to place an order, open an account, or obtain information on terms and conditions, please call our toll-free number, (800) 788-3123, between 9:00 A.M. and 5:30 P.M. PST, Monday through Friday. You may fax orders to us during all hours: (510) 658-1834.

## Mail Orders Should Be Sent to:

Grove/Atlantic, Inc.
c/o Publishers Group West
ATTN: Order Department
P.O. Box 8843
Emeryville, CA 94662

## Please Ensure that the Following Information Is Included On All Mail Orders:

1) Ship-to and bill-to addresses
2) Account number
3) Telephone and fax numbers
4) Purchase order or reference number
5) Special shipping instructions (if any)
6) Back order preferences (if any)
7) Quantity and titles of each item ordered

All orders are F.O.B. Hayward, CA.

To open an account with Publishers Group West, please submit a completed and signed credit application, including a copy of your state resale or tax exempt certificate.